PUZZLE HEROES

ANCIENT EGYPT

ANNA NILSEN

ILLUSTRATED BY
DAVID LOPEZ

W

FRANKLIN WATTS

LONDON·SYDNEY

CONTENTS

THE QUEST BEGINS

THE CHARACTERS

Granny   Zak   Leah

Meet Granny, Zak and Leah. They are space and time-travellers.

The children are learning about ancient Egypt at school and Granny thinks that they will learn a lot about Egyptian history if they visit ancient Egypt. So, one day, they gather their gear and head into the past!

THE MAP OF EGYPT

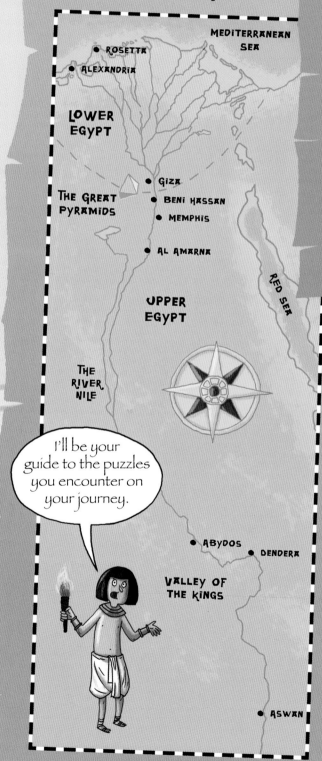

MEDITERRANEAN SEA

• ROSETTA

• ALEXANDRIA

LOWER EGYPT

THE GREAT PYRAMIDS

• GIZA

• BENI HASSAN

• MEMPHIS

• AL AMARNA

RED SEA

UPPER EGYPT

THE RIVER NILE

I'll be your guide to the puzzles you encounter on your journey.

• ABYDOS
    • DENDERA

VALLEY OF THE KINGS

• ASWAN

THE ANCIENT EGYPTIAN CURSE

The children are amazed by the Egypt of the past and gather lots of information for their school project. Then, just before they leave, Granny receives a terrifying letter. The writer tells her, 'If you want to get home alive, you must solve all the puzzles you meet on your journey or death will await you!'

ARE YOU A PUZZLE HERO?

Granny needs all the help she can get! Can you help Zak and Leah solve all the puzzles and save Granny from a terrible fate?

There are Egyptian gods to find, hieroglyphic puzzles to solve and lots to learn about the importance of death to the ancient Egyptians. But beware you don't get trapped in the pyramid maze, never to return home again!

THE NUMBERS

You will need this table of Egyptian numbers to help you work out the treasure puzzle on pages 22–23.

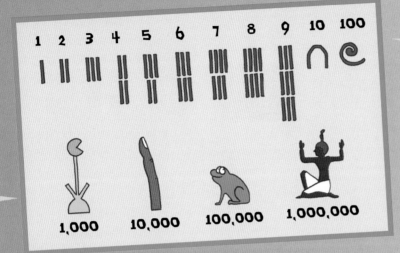

THE ALPHABET

You will need this hieroglyphic alphabet used by the Egyptians to solve the puzzle on page 22.

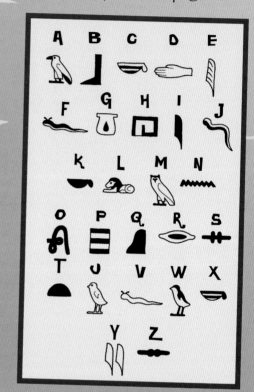

THE FAMILY TREE

You will need this family tree to help you solve the puzzle on pages 22–23. It shows you the relationships between some of the important Egyptian pharaohs (kings) and queens.

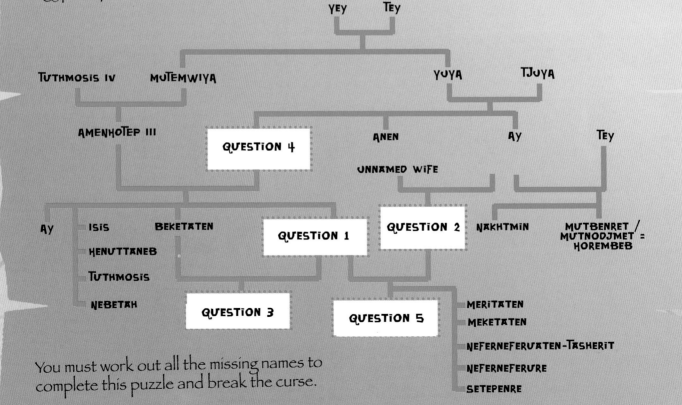

You must work out all the missing names to complete this puzzle and break the curse.

THE GIFT OF THE GODS

The ancient Egyptians believed in lots of gods and goddesses who controlled all aspects of nature and daily life. This puzzle follows a chain of gods passing on a parcel. Search each spread in turn to find the god passing the parcel to the next god in line. Then turn over to look for the god who has just received it passing it on to the next god.

Beware, there are lots of Egyptian gods in the book playing 'pass the parcel' so be sure you've found the correct god. When you reach the end of the chain you should discover who the parcel was meant for and what was in the gift. Do not get waylaid by the wrong parcels!

KHEPRI

TAWARET

TAWARET

ISIS

ISIS

HORUS

Above you can see an example group of gods and goddesses playing pass the parcel but note, this is not the group you should be following! The first god you have to find is Hapy, the god of the Nile (left). Then find the god he's passed the parcel to in the next puzzle ...

To stop the curse, the gift of the gods puzzle needs to be done in the order of the book. The other puzzles can be done in any order.

THE CHAMELEON HUNT

When they arrived in Egypt, Granny bought the children a pet chameleon at the market. It escaped. Chameleons change their colour to match their surroundings. Can you help Zak and Leah find it on each spread?

MORE TO FIND!

On every spread, you will also be challenged to find:

 Bastet – the cat goddess (take care: she has many different forms!)

 A particular god in 'Meet the gods'

 Granny's knitting passion – what has she knitted now?

SCARAB AND ANKH HUNT

The ancient Egyptians believed that charms in the shape of a scarab beetle or ankh brought good luck and warded off evil spirits.

To break the Egyptian curse you must count and check you have spotted them all throughout the book.

NAVIGATING THE NiLE

Your quest begins by the Nile, Egypt's most important river. Farmers depended on it to water their crops and fertilise the soil.

Follow the instructions to find where you need to go to break the curse.

DiRECTIONS

1. Get on your camel at A1.

2. Go south along a camel trail.

3. At the three camels, follow the trail east and south-east around an oasis.

4. Follow the trail east until you reach a boat on the Nile.

5. Sail south down the Nile to the landing point.

6. Get off at the landing point and follow the track east, north and west.

7. Sail across the Nile and follow the trail west and north to a building. Where is it?

BASTET
Bastet is the feline goddess of ancient Egyptian religion. Can you spot the black and gold statue of her?

MEET THE GODS
Hapy is god of the Nile. He has a pot belly with water plants as a crown on his head. Where is he?

GRANNY'S KNiTTING PASSION
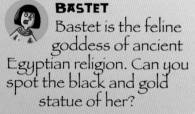
Granny has knitted something to help her cross the Nile. Follow the woollen trail to find what it is.

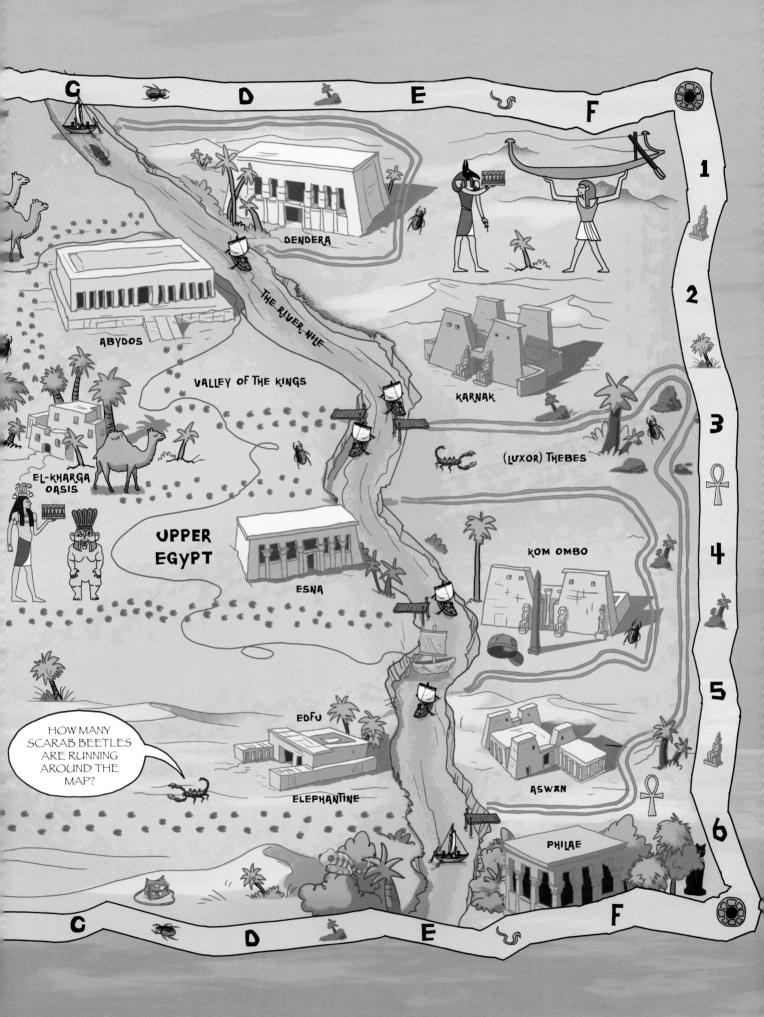

IN THE TOWN

Most Egyptian towns grew without being planned. Poor Egyptians lived in small mud houses crowded into a maze of streets.

CAMEL CHAOS

Spot the intruder! Six camels have their owners' symbols and addresses shaved into their fur. The camel owners are wearing fabric with a matching symbol. Match the owners to their camels. Work out where each person lives by matching the other symbol to the symbol on the house door. Now help Leah and Zak work out which camel and owner are the intruders!

PET HOOPOES

Egyptian children loved keeping birds called hoopoes as pets. Help Zak count them all. How many are there?

BASTET

Bastet was protector of the home and pregnant women. Where is she?

MEET THE GODS

Bes, a dwarf with the features of a lion and a human, was protector of the household. Spot him!

GRANNY'S KNITTING PASSION

Inspired by her ride to the village, Granny has knitted a large woollen object. What is it?

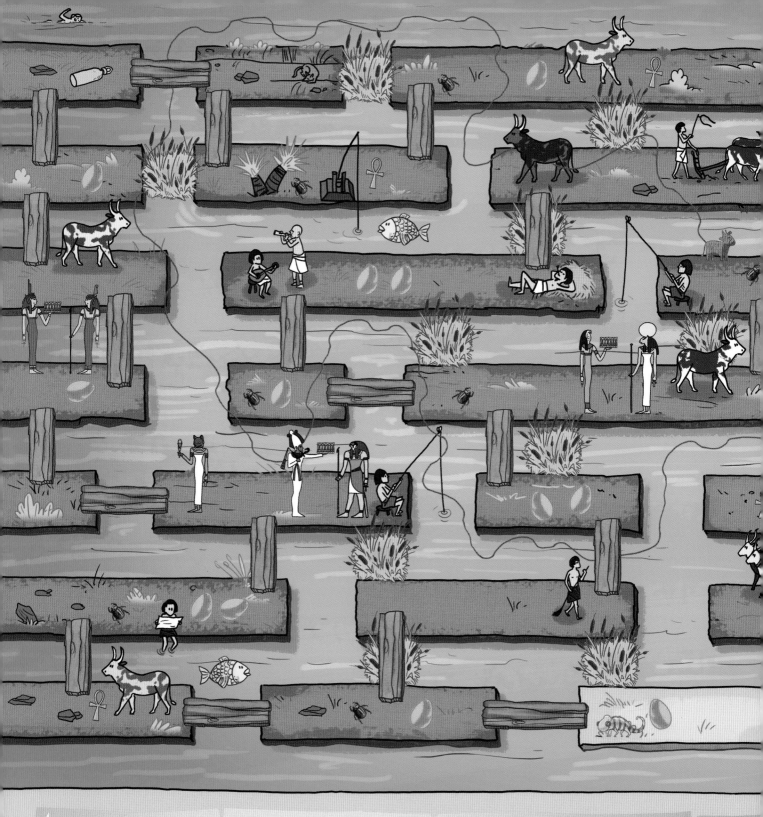

Farmers' market

Most Egyptians worked on the land and produced enough food for themselves and to pay their taxes. If they had any extra they would barter (exchange) their food for the things they wanted.

Boat £5.00

Camel £3.00

Decide whether you want to hire a boat to collect fish, or a camel to collect eggs. Go through the maze counting the fish or eggs on your chosen route, and multiply them by the price you can sell the items for at the market. Subtract the price of your transport to work out how much you have made. Find the best route for each item.

You can go under the bridges, but not through the reeds.

Duck Eggs
£1.00 each

Fish
£3.00 each

HOW MANY ANKHS CAN YOU FIND IN THE MAZE?

HOW MANY SCARAB BEETLES ARE RUNNING AROUND?

START

START

BASTET

Can you spot Bastet in the maze?

MEET THE GODS

Osiris was the god of the dead, and ruler of the underworld. Osiris was also a god of resurrection and fertility. In fact, the ancient Egyptians believed that Osiris gave them the gift of barley, one of their most important crops. Can you spot him?

GRANNY'S KNITTING PASSION

Inspired by Egyptian farming, can you spot what Granny knitted in the fields?

BATTLING BOATS

To protect their land, the Egyptians had an army to fight off attackers. They also went to war to conquer nearby countries. With its strong navy, Egypt won many sea battles.

You're at the battle of the Delta in 1175 BCE! Help the Egyptians fight off the invading Sea People. Watch out for the flying arrows! Find the ruler Ramesses III, wearing a tall blue hat and firing a bow and arrow. He will lead you to victory.

BATTLE STATIONS

Count the number of boats on each side. Who has the most?

SEA PEOPLE   EGYPTIAN

THE AFTERLIFE

The Egyptians believed in life after death and went to great trouble to prepare for death, burial and the afterlife. They believed that this process was vital to help the soul pass into the next world. Everyone who could afford to therefore made great preparations. It was essential to have a body that would not decay and a resting place where it would not be disturbed.

Journey through the rituals that prepared the Egyptians for the afterlife. Read the descriptions carefully and spot the mistake in each picture.

MEET THE GODS

Anubis was the jackal-headed god associated with mummification and the afterlife in ancient Egyptian religion.

BASTET

Can you spot Bastet with a lion-head shield in her left hand?

GRANNY'S KNITTING PASSION
What has the story of the afterlife inspired Granny to knit?

1. Dead bodies were mummified to stop them from rotting. The god Anubis, shown here laying the corpse on the funerary couch, was in charge of the ritual. The human-headed hawk represents the soul of the dead person as it leaves the body.

2. The lungs, stomach, liver and intestines were removed through a cut made on the side of the body. The organs were stored in canopic jars. One of the god Horus's four sons was represented on the lid of each jar. The human-headed Imsety protected the liver; Hapy, a baboon, guarded the lungs; Duamutef, a jackal, looked after the stomach and Qebehsenuef, a falcon, cared for the intestines. The brain was removed through the nose with a tool called a brain hook. The heart, believed to be the source of thought, was left in the body.

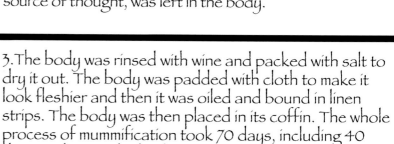

3. The body was rinsed with wine and packed with salt to dry it out. The body was padded with cloth to make it look fleshier and then it was oiled and bound in linen strips. The body was then placed in its coffin. The whole process of mummification took 70 days, including 40 days to dry out the body.

4. The funeral was held for the deceased. The body was taken in a boat, while mourners accompanied the procession, carrying treasures for the afterlife.

5. During the ceremony the priest wore a mask of Anubis. He performed a ritual of opening the mouth of the dead body to bring the mummy to life. Anubis led the soul to the afterlife. The soul, called Ba, was given offerings of food to sustain it.

HOW MANY ANKHS CAN YOU FIND?

HOW MANY SCARAB BEETLES CAN YOU FIND?

6. The Egyptians believed that, to enter your afterlife, you had to have a light heart. Light hearts were earned from doing good deeds. The spirit of the dead person had to enter the hall of judgement where the god Anubis weighed the heart against the feather of Ma'at, the goddess of truth. If the heart was lighter than the feather, the soul passed the test and entered its afterlife.

7. On the last stage of its journey, the soul could get the help of the goddess Hathor. Appearing as a cow, she carried the tired soul on her back.

PAY FOR THE PYRAMID

The pyramids were built as tombs for pharaohs (kings). Inside, the body of the dead pharaoh could travel to the afterlife, safe from thieves.

BUILDERS

The pyramid is nearly ready, but the builders need their pay. Help Zak and Leah work out the cost and pay them. There are six teams of builders. Each has a different symbol. They mark their symbol on the blocks they carve. They are paid two coins per block. Count the number of blocks each team has carved to find which team gets paid the most. The symbols are:

PAINTERS

You also need to tip the team with the most painters in it. Each team is wearing a different colour. Which of these three teams has the most painters?

BASTET
Bastet is also a daughter of Ra, the sun god. Can you spot her?

MEET THE GODS
Ptah was the god of craftsmen. Where is he?

GRANNY'S KNITTING PASSION
Find out what Granny has knitted by following the trail of wool.

TRAPPED IN A TOMB!

After death, the pharaohs were mummified and carried deep into vast tombs, such as pyramids, and buried inside a chamber.

WHERE'S GRANNY?
Granny has been left behind in the dark. Can you light the way to help her escape to daylight?

You can go under or over the maze of paths where they cross over. Beware of chambers with skeletons and mummies!

TREASURE
The Pharaoh has been buried with these gold treasures. On which route can you find the most, without going over the same junction more than once?

BASTET
Bastet is often depicted with four kittens. Can you spot them?

MEET THE GODS
Seth was the god of chaos. Where is he?

GRANNY'S KNITTING PASSION
What did Granny knit to help her escape the maze?

Do you remember the four canopic jars on page 16? Each jar was protected by a different god. Can you find the four jars?

 Hapy

 Duamutef

 Qebehsenuef

 Imsety

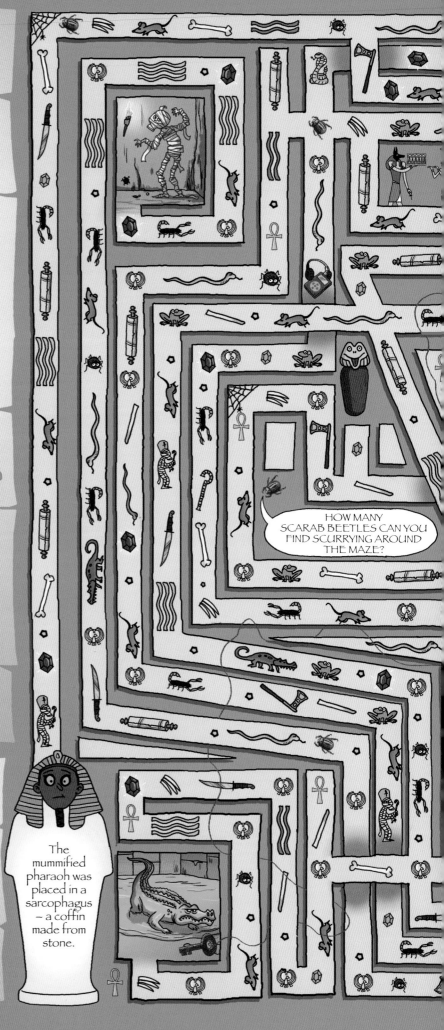

HOW MANY SCARAB BEETLES CAN YOU FIND SCURRYING AROUND THE MAZE?

The mummified pharaoh was placed in a sarcophagus – a coffin made from stone.

MATCH THE MUMMIES!

You're in a room of mummies – but who are they? Use the hieroglyph chart on page 6 to name who is in each coffin.

FAMILY TREE

Next, answer these questions to work out where these people fit on the family tree on page 6. You need to look carefully at the pictures on each coffin.

1. Who thought he was the son of the god Amun, who was represented by a sun and rays of sunshine?

2. Who was married to Akhenaten and shared the same god with a matching symbol?

3. Who was the son of Akhenaten and wore this chest decoration?

4. Tutankhamun's grandfather, Amenhotep III, had a set of scarabs inscribed for his wife and himself. Find them on the coffins to discover who Tutankhamun's grandmother was.

5. Who was Tutankhamun's wife? She wore a collar like this.

22

TREASURE TIME

Each coffin holds hidden coins. But whose coffin holds the most? Work out the number of coins in each one using the Egyptian number code on page 6. The numbers are on each coffin.

BASTET

Statues of Bastet were used to decorate items like treasure chests. Can you spot this one?

MEET THE GODS

Nephthys was a protective goddess of the dead. Where is she?

GRANNY'S KNITTING PASSION

What has Granny knitted today which is inspired by her Egyptian trip?

?

HOW MANY SCARAB BEETLES CAN YOU FIND?

KIYA'S BIRTHDAY FEAST

It's Queen Kiya's birthday and she is holding a fantastic feast in honour of Hathor, the goddess of the sky, the sun, beauty and the arts. She has prepared the goddess's favourite foods such as roast duck. But Kiya's birthday present has escaped. Find Kiya and then work out where her present has gone!

FIND KIYA
First find the friends to work out where Kiya is:

BABYU has a orange band on his head.

NIKHBET has forgotten her perfume cone and is playing a musical instrument.

TALLBAH is playing a lute.

RADAMES is turning the spit roasting-duck.

KIYA stands in the middle of the square they form, holding a box.

RUN-AWAY BIRTHDAY
Kiya's birthday present has run away. Can you find the spiny Egyptian mouse before he gets added to the feast?

BASTET
Bastet is also the goddess of joy, love and pleasure. Can you spot Bastet carrying a sistrum?

MEET THE GODS
Find Hathor, a protective goddess. She was also goddess of perfume, music and dance.

GRANNY'S KNITTING PASSION
Granny loved the music at the feast. What did she knit to the rhythm of the music?

HOW MANY SCARAB BEETLES CAN YOU FIND?

HOW MANY ANKHS CAN YOU FIND IN THE VALLEY OF THE KINGS?

HOW MANY SCARAB BEETLES ARE RUNNING AROUND THE VALLEY OF THE KINGS?

VALLEY OF THE KINGS

There are nearly forty tombs in the Valley of the Kings. Many funeral processions made their way down the valley. There would be dancers and wailing mourners carrying the things the dead person needed in the afterlife.

CANOPIC JARS

You saw the four canopic jars on page 16. Can you spot them in the crowd?

FUNERAL FIGURINES

Shabti, funeral figurines, were buried with the corpse to perform tasks in the afterlife. Many have been stolen from the tombs. Can you recover these?

BASTET
Bastet was often carved on decorative objects like this incense burner. Can you find her?

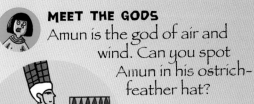

MEET THE GODS
Amun is the god of air and wind. Can you spot Amun in his ostrich-feather hat?

GRANNY'S KNITTING PASSION
Can you find what Granny knitted as a result of her trip to the Valley of the Kings?

ANSWERS

The pictures show the best routes for the mazes and where to find some of the other objects. If you can't find all the scarabs and ankhs, and the chameleon, have another go!

8-9 NAVIGATING THE NILE

MAP PUZZLE: If you follow the instructions correctly you will end up at Abydos.

- Granny has knitted a boat.
- There are 10 scarab beetles.
- There are 4 ankhs.

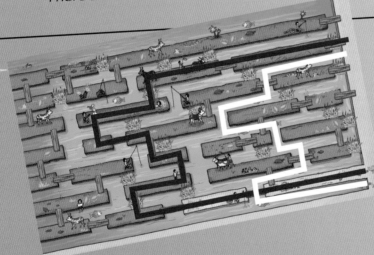

10-11 IN THE TOWN

CAMEL CHAOS: The camel with the palm tree and pyramid pattern, and the man with the pyramid pattern are the intruders.

- Pet hoopoes: there are 7 to find.
- Granny has knitted a camel.
- There are 12 scarab beetles.
- There are 5 ankhs.

12-13 FARMERS' MARKET

FARMING PUZZLE: You can collect 5 fish and make £10 (£15 minus the cost of the boat). You can collect 8 eggs and make £5 (£8 minus the cost of the camel).

- Granny has knitted a bull.
- There are 12 scarab beetles.
- There are 8 ankhs.

14-15 BATTLING BOATS

Sea people   Egyptian

LOST WEAPONS

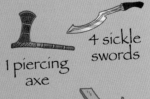

1 piercing axe   4 sickle swords

2 grappling hooks

Ramesses III

BATTLE STATIONS: There are 5 Sea People boats and 4 Egyptian (look closely at the front and back of the boats if you're not sure which is which.)

- Granny has knitted a shield.
- There are 8 scarab beetles.
- There are 9 ankhs.

16-17 THE AFTERLIFE

ERRORS IN PICTURES:

- Granny has knitted a cow.
- There are 7 scarab beetles.
- There are 6 ankhs.

1. A snake's head is pictured instead of a human's.

2. The fourth jar is a cat, not a falcon.

3. There are feathers instead of salt.

4. The vehicle is a car instead of a boat.

5. The priest is wearing the wrong mask (not Anubis).

6. Anubis is weighing a skull and a jelly rather than a heart and a feather.

7. It's a camel instead of a cow.

18-19 PAY FOR THE PYRAMID

BUILDERS' SYMBOLS:

 20   Pay the builders with the downward pointing triangle.

PAINTERS

Blue = 10   Red = 8   Green = 6

- Granny has knitted a stone block.
- There are 3 scarab beetles.
- There are 4 ankhs.

20-21 TRAPPED IN A TOMB!

TREASURE:

There are 18 gold treasures on this route.

- Granny has knitted a key.
- There are 10 scarab beetles.
- There are 15 ankhs.

22-23 MATCH THE MUMMIES!

Tutankhamun 231,538

Nefertiti 242,445

Queen Tiye 214,363

Ankhsenamun 125,237

Amenhotep III 317,211

Akhenaten 322,629

ANSWERS TO QUESTIONS:

1. Akhenaten; 2. Nefertiti; 3. Tutankhamun; 4. Queen Tiye; 5. Ankhsenamun.

- Granny has knitted a pyramid.
- There are 5 scarab beetles.
- There are 5 ankhs.

ANSWERS (CONTINUED)

24-25 KIYA'S BIRTHDAY FEAST

The friends and Kiya are marked on the picture.

- Granny has knitted a lute.
- There are 6 scarab beetles.
- There are 6 ankhs.

Nikhbet   Tallbah   Kiya   Radames   Babyu

26-27 VALLEY OF THE KINGS

- Granny has knitted a lizard.
- There are 11 scarab beetles.
- There are 7 ankhs.

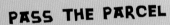 = Canopic jars

 = Funeral figurines

ONE LAST PUZZLE!

Zak and Leah each lose one piece of property on each spread. Can you go back and find all the pieces?

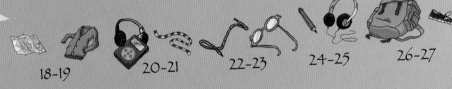

8-9   10-11   12-13   14-15   16-17

18-19   20-21   22-23   24-25   26-27

PASS THE PARCEL

If you follow through the gods correctly on each spread, you will find Amun with the parcel on the final spread with a god who has received this golden treasure.

Series editors: Melanie Palmer and Sarah Peutrill
Art director: Peter Scoulding
Designer: Matt Lilly

First published in 2013 by Franklin Watts

Text copyright © Franklin Watts 2013

Franklin Watts 338 Euston Road London NW1 3BH

Franklin Watts Australia
Level 17/207 Kent Street Sydney, NSW 2000

Dewey number: 932.01
ISBN: 978 1 4451 1908 3 (hbk)
ISBN: 978 1 4451 1910 6 (pbk)
Printed in China

Franklin Watts is a division of Hachette Children's Books,
an Hachette UK company. www.hachette.co.uk